ASSATA-GARVEY AND ME

A GLOBAL AFRICAN JOURNEY FOR CHILDREN

**Runoko Rashidi
and the Uncovering the African Past Resource Group**

ASSATA-GARVEY AND ME

A GLOBAL AFRICAN JOURNEY FOR CHILDREN

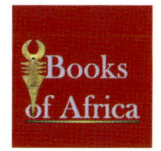

Books of Africa

Publisher:
Books of Africa Limited
16 Overhill Road
East Dulwich, London
SE22 0PH
United Kingdom

Web site: www.booksofafrica.com
Emails: admin@booksofafrica.com
sales@booksofafrica.com

Copyright : © Books of Africa 2016

ISBN : 978-0-9935036-5-8

A CIP catalogue record for this book is available from the British Library

Page layout: Opteam
contact@opteam-compo.com
production@opteam-compo.com

Printed and bound in India by Imprint Digital Ltd.

First Edition

All rights reserved. No part of this publication may be reproduced, stored in retrieval system, or transmitted in any form or by any means – electronic, mechanical, photocopying, recording or any other, – except for brief quotation in printed reviews, without the prior written permission of the publisher.

ASSATA-GARVEY AND ME
A GLOBAL AFRICAN JOURNEY FOR CHILDREN

COMPILED BY RUNOKO RASHIDI AND THE UNCOVERING
THE AFRICAN PAST RESEARCH GROUP

EDITED BY RUNOKO RASHIDI, ALTHEA COOPER,
DANNY MICHAEL, AND TERESA DOBSON

WITH CONTRIBUTIONS BY:
CARLENE AND ROBERT LAUDER, BENJAMIN LAWSON, JOYCE JOHNS,
JAEL SIMEON-GOLD, KANG MUSFASARED, DARREN MANOHARAN,
AKIKETA SHELTON, KIBAVUIDI NSIANGANI, JAHMILAH SEKHMET,
MENDECES DRAKE, OYA ADISA OSHUN AND ASSATA-GARVEY HERSELF.

Contents

Acknowledgements	7
Preface	8
Introduction	9
Assata-Garvey and me: beginning our global African journey	10
The African diaspora in Asia: the first stop from Africa!	11
The Sumerians, Elam and the queen of Sheba	11
The Dravidians	12
Enslaved Africans in Asia	13
The Siddis	14
The Dalits	14
China and Japan	15
Black Kingdoms in South East Asia	16
African people in Europe	17
Aboriginal Australia	21
Black people in the Pacific Islands	28
Africans in the Americas	32
Just the beginning!	39
Annexes	52
Annex 1: Black people all over the world	53
Annex 2: Dr Runoko's global travels map	54
Annex 3	55
Liste of captions	56
Glossary	57
For further reading	62

Acknowledgements

As with most endeavours, numerous people made important contributions. In addition to the editors and contributors already listed we would like to acknowledge Zawadi Sagna, Naomie Lara, Hamara Holt, Kodjo Daniels, Emmanuel Mah, Nigel Watt, Hubert Hintzen, Amoye Neblett, Max Walker, Kevin M. Phillips, Maximo C Ejome Esara, Kenneth McRae and the entire body of the Uncovering the African Past Research Group (UAPRG) with Runoko Rashidi.

For your ideas, your hard work, your inspiration, your love, we thank you!

Preface

In 2015 I taught an online course called Uncovering the African Past with Runoko Rashidi. The participants of the course suggested a class project and this is the result.

I had wanted for a long time to write a book for children and beginners on the Global African Community, the African Diaspora, and so this volume represents a merger of my own work with the members of what we are calling the Uncovering the African Past Research Group.

I am very proud of it. Numerous people contributed and the photos help tell the story. The activities section, in particular, is purely the work of the members of the Uncovering the African Past Research Group.

Assata-Garvey and Me is a narrative and pictorial story of the global journeys of African people as told by me to my daughter, Assata-Garvey. But Assata-Garvey could be your child. She could be all of our children who need to know the global history of African people, a history that does not begin with enslavement or servitude or colonization. It starts at the beginning of human history, at the beginning of our history, at the beginning of our story.

Few books written for children tell the story of African people from ancient times.

This work is about the African people who in ancient times began to move out of Africa to many other parts of the world. These movements of people, called migrations, started from Africa more than 100,000 years ago. Some of the movements were voluntary and others, as we well know, were not. Five major regions are featured here: Asia, Europe, Australia, the Pacific Islands, and the Americas. All of these areas where people of Africa reached were settled in both ancient and modern times.

Runoko Rashidi
Paris, France
June 2016

Introduction

In this book we have chosen to start at the beginning.

Africa is where human life began. Since Africa is the birthplace of the first humans, it is often called the motherland or Mother Africa. As people learned to live and work together, they formed human cultures. They learned to grow food to eat. They learned to build shelter or homes to protect themselves. They formed families to teach their children. They expressed their talents through art and music and dance. They made tools from materials around them and all these innovations and efforts helped them to survive. This kind of organized way of living came to be known as civilization.

As African people travelled to distant, new places, their cultures and all they had learned about life went with them. In their new locations, they used their African cultures to establish themselves and survive in their various environments. The communities to which Africans migrated are called the Global African Community or, simply put, the African Diaspora.

Some groups of the people and their great leaders in each region are highlighted in this book. But there are many more than can fit into these pages.

Some of the ancient people of Africa who migrated to other parts of the world include the people called the San and the Batwa. These are very ancient peoples, probably the first people on earth that we know of. The world knows these ancient African people as *Bushmen* and *Pygmies* but we will continue to call them by their rightful names.

Now we prepare to leave Africa to follow the main paths of the migrations and movements that make up the Global African Community. We are going to follow our ancestors to all parts of the world – to Asia, Europe, Australia, the Pacific Islands, and the Americas.

Assata-Garvey and me: beginning our global African journey

Good morning Dad! How are you?

Good morning Assata-Garvey, I'm fine, just a little tired. How are you?

I'm fine, Dad, I'm so happy you're back! That was another long trip. I missed you!
Did you find what you were looking for?

Oh yes! I found a lot! I visited some Black communities and found some museums.

Tell me about it Dad! I want to hear everything! And you can show me some pictures too! Let's start right now!

Okay, Assata-Garvey, let me tell you and let me show you. In fact, since you want to hear so much, let me tell you about a lot of my African journeys around the world and the different places where Black people have been and are today. But one thing though; since you have already travelled to Africa several times, let me take you through what people call the African Diaspora and what I call the Global African community.

Now you know your dad. I am a historian and an anthropologist, a writer and a world traveller and once I get started I am not going to want to stop!

Some other brothers and sisters, all friends and students of mine, helped compile this information. They also added some activities to help you learn even more and remember what you learned! They all have children of their own, just like you, and they are all interested in travel and the conditions of Black people wherever we are in the world.

So while taking you around the world with me I have to tell you that this is not just my work. This is all of our work. And we will definitely meet some of our most important and illustrious ancestors on our journey.

If there are any words or names you don't understand, just look at the glossary at the end of the book!

Okay Assata-Garvey, here we go!

Let's begin our Global African Journey!

The African diaspora in Asia: the first stop from Africa!

Assata-Garvey, migrations out of Africa to Asia probably began 100,000 years ago, forming the many groups of Black people we see today in the area. We call them the Diminutive Africoids or Small Black People. The Small Black People include:

- Jarawa and Onge people of the Andaman and Nicobar Islands,
- Semang people of Malaysia,
- Ngok people of Thailand and,
- Ati, Aeta, Agi, and numerous groups in the Philippines.

These people are the settlers from probably the first migration out of Africa. The Small Black People are known to have short stature, dark skin, woolly hair and little body hair.

The Jawara people are among the darkest skinned people on earth and their isolation from other civilizations has maintained their distinct physical characteristics.

Wow, Dad! Our people were traveling to all these places 100,000 years ago. Amazing!

Yes princess, it is amazing, and there is even more.

The Sumerians, Elam and the queen of Sheba

About five-thousand years ago, the Sumerians, in what is now southern Iraq, built the first great civilization in Asia. They called themselves the Blackheaded people and helped introduce astronomy, mathematics, and pharmacies. They built huge stepped structures now called *ziggurats*. From a distance the ziggurats look a lot like the stepped pyramid that the African genius Imhotep designed in Kmt. One of the great leaders of the Sumerians was Gudea. Another legendary leader of the Sumerians was the woman known as Kubaba.

The next great civilization in Southwest Asia is called Elam. Elam is nearly as old as Sumer and existed in the country that is now called Iran. It lasted for more than a thousand years beginning about 2800 BCE. The greatest city in Elam was called Susa.

In the south west part of the Arabian Peninsula (now known as Yemen) arose the Kingdom of Saba. This was a land probably ruled by the famous woman known as Makeda to some and Bilqis to others. The world knows her as the Queen of Sheba!

The Dravidians

One of the earliest and perhaps the first people to inhabit India were the Dravidians. They are Black people with different hair textures, generally wavy to straight. In addition, they built the mighty city of Harappa in the Indus Valley that ruled what is now Pakistan and northern India over five thousand years ago. These people now mostly live in areas of southern India and Sri Lanka.

1. Runoko Rashidi and a Black man from Bangladesh, in Muscat, Oman
Photo credit: Runoko Rashidi

Around the sixth century, about fifteen hundred years ago, martial arts spread from southern India to China. Martial arts is now a large part of Eastern Asian culture. There was a Tamil prince from South India who became a monk named Daruma Bodhidharma. He was responsible for the spread of martial arts in these regions.

The Chola and Pallava Empires of the Tamil country also influenced the designs of many temples and statues we see of people of African origin around Southeast Asia. A clear example of this is at the temple complex called Angkor Wat in Cambodia.

2. One of the entrances to the city of Angkor Thom at Siem Reap, Cambodia
Photo credit: Runoko Rashidi

The Gonds, Adivasis, along with others in India and Veddas of Sri Lanka are known to be more ancient than the Dravidian peoples of the region. They look a lot like the indigenous or aboriginal populations of Australia.

Enslaved Africans in Asia

There is also a history of enslaved Africans in south west and south Asia. They were brought to Asia by the people called Arabs and were taken from places in Africa like today's Sudan, Ethiopia, Kenya, Tanzania and Mozambique. The Arab capture and sale of African people in Asia went on for hundreds of years.

In Iraq these Africans were called Zanj. You can still see their name in the island of Zanzibar in East Africa. From 868 to 883 the Zanj carried out the largest revolt of enslaved people in history. It is called the "Revolt of the Zanj!

In Turkey I met the descendants of enslaved Africans who were carried from Sudan, Egypt and Ethiopia more than a hundred years ago during the time of the Ottoman Empire.

In Pakistan the descendants of enslaved Africans are called Sheedis. In India they are known as Siddis.

The Siddis

Siddis, or Habshi, are the descendants of mainly eastern Africans. They were brought to India and Pakistan by Arab merchants in medieval times. During this time, they were recruited as personal bodyguards, servants, and musicians. Some even became powerful generals serving their kings! They now mainly live in self-contained communities. These people look identical to their brothers and sisters in Africa.

The Dalits

Another group of people in India we cannot leave out are the Dalits. They have been called the Black Untouchables of India. They are the most oppressed people in the world. They are taught that even their shadows and the sounds of their voices will cause pollution to other people!

That's awful! I'm glad that's a thing of the past.

No, Assata-Garvey, unfortunately it still happens. It is our responsibility to make it a thing of the past.

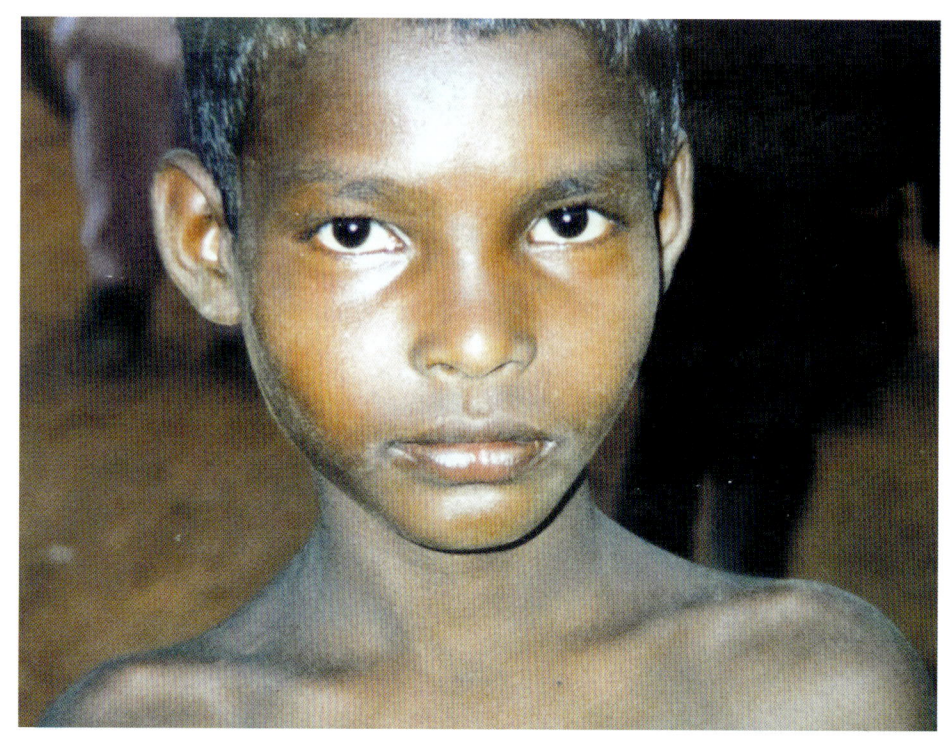

3. A Munda boy in Orissa, India
Photo credit: Runoko Rashidi

China and Japan

The records tell us that the first people of China were Black and the African beginnings in Asia can still be seen throughout the continent in the artefacts and monuments left by these people. In the early period, during the time of the Shang Dynasty some of the art shows Black people. The Tang Dynasty was the classical period of literature and art in China. They have what appears to be Black, curly-haired acrobats. The Yuan Dynasty of China was started by the Mongol conqueror Kublai Khan. There were a number of Black people in prominent positions during the time of this dynasty.

Two proverbs in Japan have been used to suggest an African presence. One goes, "For a samurai to be brave he must have a bit of black blood." Another goes, "To make a good samurai half the blood in one's veins must be black." There is also the tradition that the first Shogun of Japan was Black! His name was Sakanouye Tamuramaro.

What is a Shogun, dad?

The Shoguns were the military rulers of early Japan. The ancestor Sakanouye was a man with rich dark brown skin much like ours. When he was young, his family moved from Korea to Japan. As an adult, he became a skilled military general and successfully guarded and protected the emperor's court from the year 794 until 811 CE. He led his army with intelligence, strength, honour and bravery. As long as he was in charge, no one was able to invade Japan. It is great ancestors like these that show us that we can be great leaders and achieve anything that we decide we want to achieve.

Assata-Garvey, I have often seen such strength and bravery in you.

4. An Africoid figurine – perhaps an acrobat or a dancer from the Tang Dynasty in China. In the Smithsonian Collection in Washington
Photo credit: Runoko Rashidi

Black Kingdoms in South East Asia

In south east Asia there were great Black kingdoms in Thailand, Cambodia and Vietnam.

More than a thousand years ago in Thailand, the people created images of the Buddha with distinct African features. This period in Thailand is called the Dvaravati Period.

In Cambodia you had an early Black kingdom called Funan. Then came the classical civilization in Southeast Asian history built by the people called Khmers. This civilization was called Angkor.

In Vietnam was the Cham civilization. It lasted more than a thousand years! You can find many African-looking artistic pieces of Cham in the great museums of the world!

5. A Buddha from early Thailand - Musee Guimet
Photo credit: Runoko Rashidi

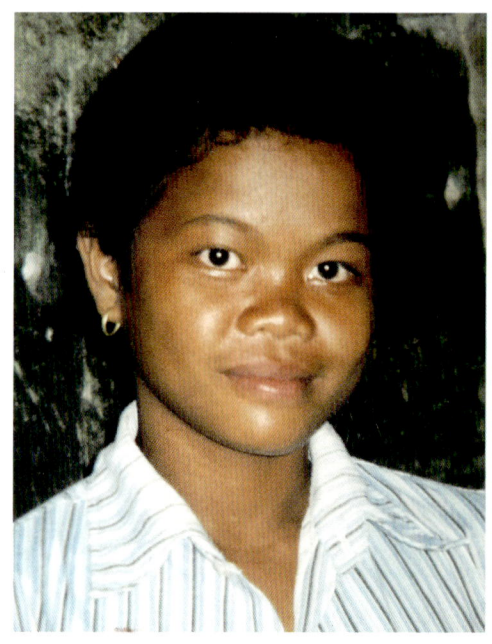

6. A Khmer girl in Siem Reap, Cambodia
Photo credit: Runoko Rashidi

I'm glad you brought your camera and took some really beautiful photos of the art pieces in the museum! And look at these pictures of our people in the African diaspora of Asia. I didn't know we journeyed to all those places. Do you think Africans also travelled to this part of the world? African people in Europe?

Yes, of course they did, Assata-Garvey. Let's continue our journey into the land of Europe now!

African people in Europe

Here, we will learn about African people's impact in this part of the world. It was at least 40,000 years ago when they were migrating into Europe. These people, of course, were Black.

You also have images of Black people thousands of years old on the island of Crete in the Mediterranean Sea. Crete is important to us because it is the first known great civilization of Europe. Crete is a part of Greece now.

Greece is a European country that sits directly north of Egypt on the Mediterranean Sea. Most everybody has heard of Greece. It was the height of European civilization and culture. As you get older you will hear the names of Homer, Plato, Socrates, Aristotle and Alexander. But we rarely hear about the famous Black people in the history of Greece. One such man was Aesop, a great story teller. Another man was a great general in the army of Alexander the Great. This Black man was Clitus the Niger or Clitus the Black.

Even bigger than Greece was the Roman Empire, centered around the city called Rome. Rome is found in the country known as Italy and the leaders of the Roman Empire were called *caesars*. The most famous of them was Julius Caesar, who invaded Africa and married the Queen of Egypt, Cleopatra VII.

In the year 193 a Black man from Libya named Septimius Severus started an African dynasty in Rome. It was named after him and is known as the Severan Dynasty. This African dynasty lasted for forty-three years.

7. The head of the African emperor of Rome Septimius Severus
Photo credit: Runoko Rashidi

8. A Black person from the Etruscan civilization of early Italy
Photo credit: Runoko Rashidi

In ancient Rome there were African senators, African gladiators, African popes, African saints, African artists and African writers. The most famous of these writers was Terence. Called Terence Afer, this was the Black man who gave us the expression: "I am a man and reckon that nothing human is alien to me!" He also gave us the famous expression, "Where there is life there is hope!"

When the Roman Empire fell apart, Europe went into a "Dark Age". At this time (around the year 711), a new wave of northern Africans came into Europe to help save the people from their miserable conditions. They called these Black people "Moors". The Moors brought the light to Europe's dark period. They reintroduced science and learning. They even introduced to Europe the game of chess! The word "moor" means "black" or "scorched."

You also find real Black knights from this period. The most famous Black knight in Europe was a man who was also considered to be a "Saint". His name was Saint Maurice and he was born in Egypt, and lived during the Roman times in Europe about seventeen-hundred years ago!

9. Saint Maurice – the knight in shining armour
Photo credit: Runoko Rashidi

10. Runoko Rashidi and a portrait of Alexander Sergeivich Pushkin in Moscow, Russia
Photo credit: Runoko Rashidi

In the legend of the "round table" of King Arthur of Britain there was a heroic Black knight called Sir Morien. He was described as "black as a raven," and there was "nothing white about him but his teeth!"

During this time, religious images, we call them *icons*, called "Black Madonnas" became very popular in Europe.

Black Madonna? I think I have heard that before, but can you please tell me what that is?

A Madonna is a great woman who is a perfect mother. The Black Madonna is always shown holding her son, the infant Jesus. Black Madonnas were always considered to be a sign of good luck. In fact, many pray to them for miracles!

11. A Black Madonna and Child in Prague, Czech Republic
Photo credit: Runoko Rashidi

12. Canada Toronto fine arts (17)
Photo credit: Runoko Rashidi

13. A bronze bust of a Moorish girl in Italy
Photo credit: Runoko Rashidi

14. Runoko Rashidi and with a group of Black women in Turkey
Photo credit: Runoko Rashidi

Did you know that England also had a queen of African heritage?

Really? A Black Queen of England?

Yes, Assata-Garvey. The first queen of African heritage in England was named Sophia Charlotte. Queen Charlotte, the wife of King George III, was a direct descendant from Margarita de Castro y Sousa, a Moorish branch of the Portuguese Royal House. She was well read and had interest in the fine arts. Queen Charlotte helped to establish Kew Gardens, the world's largest collection of exotic living plants. She was responsible for bringing the Strelitzia Reginae, a flowering plant from South Africa.

Later you have famous men of African heritage in Europe.

The most famous African in Austria during this time of Angelo Soliman. He was a great educator and a friend of the composer Mozart. In Sweden the most famous African was Adolph Badin. He wrote a book about his life and had a personal library of eight-hundred books! Both Soliman and Badin lived about two-hundred years ago.

Abraham Hanibal who lived In Russia was born in what is now Cameroon around 1699. Hanibal was eventually adopted as the godson of Russian Emperor Peter the Great and achieved wealth and distinction. He is also famous as the African ancestor of the great national writer of Russia, Alexander Sergeivich Pushkin. Alexander Pushkin had a vocabulary of 20,000 words. He wrote many poems and short stories, and helped create the present day Russian language.

Alexandre Dumas was the son of a Black man born in Haiti and who became an important general in the French army. Alexandre Dumas wrote the famous books "*The Three Musketeers,*" "*The Man in the Iron Mask,*" and "*The Count of Monte Cristo.*" He gave us the expression "One for all and all for one!"

I love that expression!

Yes, me too. It is the reason why I enjoy meeting and talking with Black people throughout the diaspora. We learn how much we have in common as one people.

Today there are African people in probably every country in Europe!

This is really fun! Where will we journey next?

Aboriginal Australia

Assata-Garvey, we are going to Australia now. I have been there ten times. I love the Black people there. So here we go. Would you mind if we invite some friends?

Okay, Dad! That will be fun!

Fasten your seatbelts young brothers and sisters. Our next stop is Australia! The root of the name "Australia" is "austral", meaning "south" or "southerly". "Australia" is a European name that means "Great South Land".

There were many migrations to Australia in ancient times. In fact, a lot of us believe that the Aboriginal Australians are the first descendants of the first migration from Africa. These Africans began migrating to Australia 75,000 years ago. They were migrants who came from Africa to Asia, then from Asia to Australia. These migrations took place over thousands of years, and covered many thousands of miles.

The story of these migrations is what the "scientific" evidence tells us. Yet, many of the Aboriginal Australians themselves believe that they have always been there. Some of them actually believe that Africans first came from Australia! One thing is for certain, we are members of the same human family! They are our brothers and sisters!

Australia was made up of many different groups of Black people with different names. Today, they are known as Aboriginal Australians, Indigenous Australians, or Black Australians. In Australia, they are called Blackfellas.

We are now landing in Tasmania. I want you to meet a very important woman. She is actually an ancestor who will be your guide as we learn about our history and present time in this fascinating part of the world.

Let's meet our special ancestor. Welcome to Tasmania! Everyone, this is Truganini. She is the last full-blood Tasmanian. Tasmania is an island off the southeast coast of Australia. You will learn more about her people later.

But first, I want her to tell you about how they lived in Australia.

Does anyone have any questions?

"What kind of foods did you eat?"

There was no type of food production as we know of today. Yams, fruits and nuts were important foods for us. Yams were harvested with special digging sticks usually by our women and children. Our men and boys hunted animals or went fishing.

There were tools for food preparation. The oldest grinding stone found in western New South Wales, part of Australia, is about 30,000 years old. Sharp stone blades were used for cutting, and stone axes for chopping things. Water was carried in bowls made from large shells, animal skins and tree bark.

"How did you take care of sick people?"

Our medicines were everywhere around us in certain tree barks, plant leaves and seeds. We soaked, steamed or boiled them to get our medicines.

"Did you use a bow and arrow?"

We used a *woomera,* a tool that guided the arrow. It was like holding a paper plane by the tail to make it fly.

We also had the returning boomerang for hunting and self-defence. There were shields for protection.

"Did children play with toys?"

Oh, yes they had many toys! Our most popular toys were the cross boomerang, the spinning top, and propellers. The best part was that we made the toys ourselves!

Our children loved to play, but we had to pay attention to other daily chores as well. We did not tell the time with clocks as you do today. The sun guided us through our day from daybreak, sunrise, morning, midday, afternoon, and sunset ending our day.

We did not count months with numbers. The moon and the stars were our calendar. From one new moon to the next was a month which equals 29 days. We also knew when certain foods were available, when certain animals would have babies, and when seasons would change. It was written in the stars.

What does "written in the stars" mean?

Watching the stars move was how we knew when these things would happen. Sadly, we lost most of our knowledge of these things after the arrival of Europeans. This means you will never truly know and enjoy all of our ancient knowledge. There is an African saying: "When an elder dies a library burns to the ground". Many of our people died in a short period of time. I will explain more about what happened to our people after the next subject, our spirituality.

In Australia, spirituality is very important to our Indigenous people. Spirituality is the way my people peacefully live in harmony with each other and nature. It is the belief in our Creator Beings. Mother Earth is sacred to our identity and culture. The land is the main focus and base for our beliefs.

There were no writing systems or books, yet our artworks show some of the symbols used to tell our story. There are places that are especially important to us. We call these places our sacred sites or holy places. Sacred sites are made from things in nature that has a connection with the Ancestor Beings in the past, or was chosen by our ancestors. Things like trees, rocks, mountains, waterholes, or parks are examples of our sacred sites.

15. Runoko Rashidi with two Indigenous Elders in Townsville, Queensland, Australia
Photo credit: Runoko Rashidi

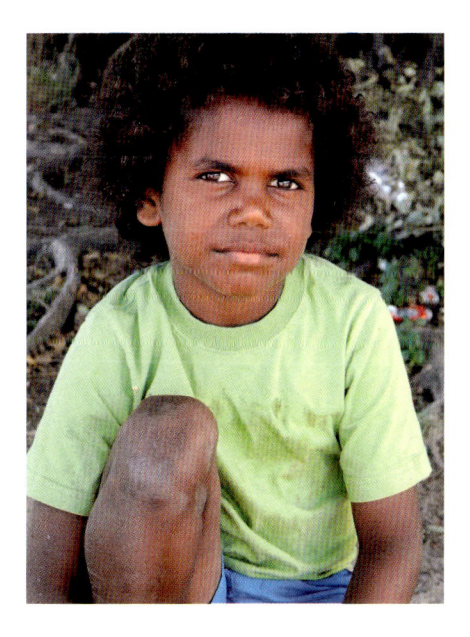

16. An Aboriginal Australian boy on Palm Island, Queensland, Australia
Photo credit: Runoko Rashidi

17. An Indigenous Australian woman on Palm Island Queensland – Australia
Photo credit: Runoko Rashidi

These sites were created in The Dreaming or Dreamtime. The Dreaming was from the land, and Europeans did not destroy it. It is a living way of life for our people. We are protecting it and the land.

Each generation was taught the stories of creation by our elders, and have to remember them throughout their lives. These were stories of the knowledge of how to live and survive in the harsh lands of Australia. Some sacred knowledge is kept secret and only taught to a few who are chosen by the elders. Some information is also only for women. There are also things that are only taught to men. Ceremonies were performed to preserve the life of the land.

During the Dreaming, ancestral spirits came to earth and created the land, the animals and plants. The stories tell how the ancestral spirits moved through the land creating rivers, lakes and mountains.

Today we know the places where the ancestral spirits have been and where they came to rest. They tell how people came to Australia and how the groups connect throughout Australia. There are explanations about how people learned languages, dances, and how they came to know about fire.

We celebrate our dreaming stories by singing songs about the dreamtime, chanting and performing ceremonies and rituals. We also act in dreamtime plays, as well as dance in routines that show the movement of our Creator Being. During our different ceremonies and rituals we always paint our bodies with bright colours and traditional designs. Each of them is connected to that specific ceremony, our laws and spirituality. We also wear our handmade jewellery made from things given to us by Mother Earth like plants, feathers, and nuts. We have lived this way for over 50,000 years.

My dear child, you are very special. You come from a long line of beautiful people, with skin like the evening skies, and eyes that shine like the stars. Never forget that we are one with our great land, the animals, and the ancestors. One day you will be part of the Dreamtime.

Do you think we could have our own dreamtime ceremony!

Well, there are enough of us here for a celebration so I don't see why not. I have more to tell you though. Afterwards, we can celebrate the dreamtime with a special song.

Aboriginal Australians lived in peace and harmony for tens of thousands of years. That changed when thirteen British ships landed in 1788 in a place now called Botany Bay. It is located near Sydney in New South Wales. On these ships were mostly prisoners, sent to Australia as punishment. It was a very dangerous time for the indigenous people.

At that time there were about a million Black people in Australia with over 500 indigenous nations. Their lands were taken from them by these invaders. New South Wales was turned into a prison colony. This also happened in the other parts of Australia: Queensland, Victoria, Western Australia, and South Australia.

Today, Aboriginal Australians are a very small number of the total Australian population. They fought hard to stop the British, but most of them were killed. The European invaders even used disease warfare to overpower and kill our Indigenous brothers and sisters. The greatest resistance leader who fought for our people in the New South Wales area was a brother named Pemulwuy.

In Tasmania, I saw the destruction of many of my people by the British. There is a myth that all Aboriginal Tasmanians were killed. This is not true! Aboriginal Tasmanian women were captured by British seal hunters and enslaved. My mother was killed, my sister was stolen and killed, and my fiancé was killed trying to protect me from being kidnapped and enslaved. About 5,000 British people and soldiers formed a straight line called the "Black Line" and marched across the island, killing or capturing my people.

In 1834, the last Tasmanian Aborigines were sent to a mission on a small island off the northern coast called "Flinders Island". Children were born here, and these are the Aboriginal Tasmanians of today. These sisters and brothers are very light-skinned with different colours of straight hair. The majority of us did not survive there. I was among the thirty-four people who did survive, and was allowed by the government to return to Tasmania in 1847.

In all parts of Australia, Aboriginal Australian children were taken from their parents. They are called the Stolen Generation. These stolen children were raised like slaves in local orphanages and concentration camps. It was believed that my race would not survive. We were not treated as humans, and were officially regarded as plants and animals, until the government of Australia officially considered us human in 1967. One of these camps in Tasmania was called Oyster Cove. It was a wet, cold, and swampy place. There are many trees there. We have photos of the last full-blood Aboriginal Tasmanians at Oyster Cove, and children of the Stolen Generation. Today Aboriginal Australians are haunted by high unemployment and imprisonment, deaths in prison, poor health, and domestic violence. Life for my people is very hard. We are now the adult children from the Stolen Generation.

Yet, our resistance to European domination has never ended! In 1972, the Aboriginal flag was first flown at the Australian Tent Embassy on the lawns of Parliament House in Canberra. Canberra is the capital of Australia. At this makeshift embassy it was decided that the Aboriginal nation needed a flag. Several designs were presented. This flag, designed by Harold Thomas, an Aboriginal activist and artist from Central Australia, was selected. The three parts of the flag represent the sun, the earth and the people.

We have had two chapters of Marcus Garvey's Universal Negro Improvement Association (UNIA) and African Communities League (ACL) in Australia.

There were sit-ins and Freedom Rides. There was a Black Power Movement and a Black Panther Party established in Brisbane, Australia in 1975.

Today, the government is attempting to steal the mineral rich lands from 150 Indigenous Australian communities and are destroying our homes. Our people of these communities have no place to go. We belong to the land, so we will fight for our freedom!

Thank you brother Runoko, Assata-Garvey and all of you young brothers and sisters. It was my pleasure to be your guide on this journey of my beautiful country, Australia.

There is so much more to learn about all of the Blacks who migrated, lived, loved, fought, died, and survived throughout the diaspora. I bid you farewell as you journey to your next stop, the Pacific Islands, with a song which tells the story of the Indigenous Aborigines. Join in as we sing this special song for our Dreamtime celebration!

Spiritual Song of The Aborigine
(Written by Hyllus Noel Maris)

I am a child of the Dreamtime People,
Part of this land, like the gnarled gumtree I am the river, softly singing,
Chanting our songs on my way to the sea.
My spirit is the dust-devils,
Mirages, that dance on the plain.
I'm the snow, the wind and the falling rain.
I'm part of the rocks and the red desert earth,
Red as the blood that flows in my veins.
I am eagle, crow and snake that glides
Through the rainforest that clings to the mountainside.
I awakened here when the earth was new.
There was emu, wombat, kangaroo,
No other man of a different hue.
I am this land
And this land is me I am Australia.

That was amazing and sad!! Dad, do you believe we can figure out a way to help our brothers and sisters who are still suffering in Australia?

I believe we can do anything we come together to achieve, Assata-Garvey.
Are you ready to travel with me to the Pacific Islands for the next location of our next journey?

Yes, let's go, Dad!

Black people in the Pacific Islands

Assata-Garvey, one of my favourite places in the world is the Pacific Islands. I just love it there!

The Pacific Islands are made up of more than 2000 islands. They are located on three big chains of islands in the Pacific Ocean. One island chain is called **Melanesia.** That means "the Black Islands" and it takes it name from the Black people who live there.

One group of islands in Melanesia is called **New Caledonia**. The original people there are called Kanak. New Caledonia was colonized by the French and they are still there. Chief Atai was a very brave freedom fighter in New Caledonia in the nineteenth century. There is still a strong independence movement there today.

Then there is Vanuatu. The name Vanuatu means "land eternal". You remember that I was caught in the massive cyclone in Vanuatu? "Global warming", was the cause said President of Vanuatu, Baldwin Longsdale. You remember how I told you that the people of Vanuatu were so helpful and supportive of me? It is something I will never forget. Then I have been to Fiji twice. I love it there. Everybody says that they come from Africa. They also drink a beverage called kava. It tastes like muddy water but I drank a lot of kava!

18. A young boy with blond hair in Fiji
Photo credit: Runoko Rashidi

The Solomon Islands are in the northern part of Melanesia and are close to the Buka and Bougainville islands in Papua New Guinea. I hope to visit the Solomons very soon.

By far the biggest of the islands of Melanesia is New Guinea. And New Guinea itself is divided into two parts. The eastern half is the country of Papua New Guinea. I went there in 2008. I loved it. Papua New Guinea is said to have 5000 languages. When I was there I visited the capital of Papua New Guinea, called Port Moresby. I also visited East New Britain, and the Buka and Bougainville Islands. I learned a lot and really enjoyed meeting the people.

The western half of New Guinea is West Papua. West Papua is currently occupied by Indonesia and the Indonesian government is doing terrible things to the people here. The most famous activist in West Papua is Chief Benny Wenda of the Dani people. He lives in exile in Oxford, England. I met Benny in Senegal in West Africa a few years ago and we became good friends. His children call me Uncle Runoko. Benny told me that Black people migrated from Africa to New Guinea about 30,000 years ago!

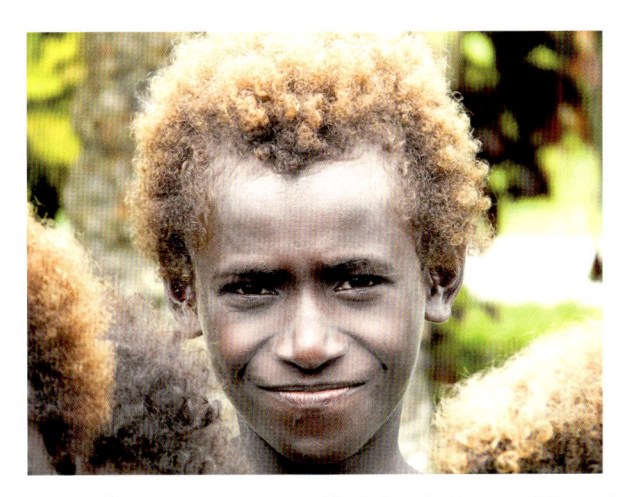

19. A young boy on Bougainville Island, Papua New Guinea
Photo credit: Runoko Rashidi

I have a lot of beautiful pictures of Melanesia and the people of Melanesia. Some of the people of Melanesia have blond hair. Yes, there are Black people with natural blond hair! In the nineteenth century the people of Melanesia were the victims of slave raiding. This was called "blackbirding." Many of these Black people ended up in Australia working on the sugar cane plantations there. It was very sad.

The second island chain in Pacific is called Micronesia. Micronesia means "the small islands." I have also been to Micronesia several times. I have been to Guam, Chuuk, Yap, Kosrae and Palau. Chuuk was very nice but Palau was definitely the best place in Micronesia. The people were so friendly to me!

The third island chain in the Pacific is called **Polynesia**. Polynesia means "many islands." It covers a huge area! All the way from New Zealand to Tahiti, Tonga and Samoa. The people of New Zealand are called Maori. Their name for New Zealand is Aotearoa.

The most famous part of Polynesia is Hawaii. I have visited Polynesia a lot of times, once to New Zealand but several times to Hawaii. I used to teach at the University at Hawaii at Manoa. I have lectured there many times and also at universities in other parts of Hawaii. When you see the pictures of the first great king of Hawaii, Kamehameha the Great, you are looking at a Black man!

20. Young boys on Buka Island, Papua New Guinea
Photo credit: Runoko Rashidi

The original people of the Pacific Islands are Black people. In some of the islands of Melanesia, like Fiji, Buka Island, the Solomon Islands, and West Papua the people say that they come from Africa. And they are very proud of it.

Assata-Garvey, someday I want to take you to the Pacific Islands. It is one of the most beautiful places on earth!

I would love to travel with you by boat to visit as many islands in the Pacific as we can! It would be exciting to see all of these places, and meet the children in these photos that you've shared with me. Maybe we can both visit Solomon Islands together for the first time!

That would be very a special trip with you, Assata-Garvey.

Now, where would you like to go next?

Let's go to the Americas, Dad!

21. A statue of King Kamehemeha the Great in Hilo, Hawaii
Photo credit: Runoko Rashidi

Africans in the Americas

Now, take a journey with me as we look at ancient arrivals of Black people in the Americas. The Americas extend from the North Pole to the tip of South America.

Scientists say the first known person in the Americas was Luzia, a Black woman whose skull was found in Brazil. It is anywhere from 11,000 to 30,000 years old. She was named after Lucy or Dinknesh, the ancient bones from Ethiopia. Because of DNA analysis, we know that humanity began in Africa and stretched to the far corners of the earth, including the Americas.

About 4000 years ago appeared a culture called the **Olmec**. The Olmecs are important as the first great civilization of the Americas. The Olmec presence shows up in three areas in the Gulf of Mexico: San Lorenzo, La Venta and Tres Zapotes. The most interesting find among the Olmec are giant stone heads. There are seventeen of these large African-looking heads carved from basalt stone.

The faces and braids on these stones make them look like African people. One of the heads has braids in the back. Olmec means "rubber people". Some scholars think that a few hundred Africans lived among the Olmec. They introduced science, writing, engineering and agriculture to the Olmec people. The Olmec were not an African people, but Africans left their mark on the Olmec culture. The great stone heads were a tribute to the African contribution to Olmec society.

The Olmec civilization lasted from about 2000 BCE. They were replaced by the **Mayan civilization**. But even the Mayan civilization appears to have had an African presence. We see many images among the ancient Maya that appear to be Black.

22. One of the Olmec Heads in Mexico
Photo credit: Runoko Rashidi

Mansa Abubakari II was the ninth mansa or emperor of the Mali Empire in West Africa. It is written that in the 1300s, Abubakari stepped down from his throne to explore the world. He built more than a thousand ships and sailed with many men and supplies across the Atlantic Ocean. Although most books claim that Europeans discovered America, it is documented that "Africa's greatest Explorer", Mansa Abubakari II, came to America more than two-hundred years before Columbus.

The movements and appearances of African people in the early Americas went on for thousands of years. Who were these ancient sisters and brothers? As for the Olmec, I believe that these massive heads with African features represent a dynasty of African kings who ruled over ancient Mexico!

Assata-Garvey, I know that you must have heard of Columbus? For a long time people claimed that he had "discovered" America! Well even Columbus said he heard stories about Africans in the Americas. In 1513 the Spanish sailor Balboa reported that he saw Black people that he called "Ethiopians" in Panama, in Central America, at a place called Darrien.

Where did they go? What happened next?

What came next interrupted history. It is called **slavery**. The Transatlantic Slave Trade is where we venture to now. After thousands of years of the African presence in American civilization our progress was halted. For hundreds of years our ancestors were hunted like animals. Many of them died in this great crime against humanity. This is how our progress was stopped.

As we continue our journey through the Americas, you should know that many Africans resisted enslavement. So now let's begin a new phase of the African story in the Americas – enslavement and resistance. Let me introduce you to a few men and women, great ancestors, who died so that we could live free.

Perhaps the greatest freedom fighters against the enslavement and oppression of African people in the Americas were the people called *Maroons*. The Maroons refused to accept enslavement and formed their own communities. Some of the most famous of these communities were in Mexico, Brazil and Suriname. In Mexico the Maroons were led by Gaspar Yanga, in Brazil by Zumbi Dos Palmares, while in Suriname one of the greatest leaders was called Boni.

23. A little Saamaka girl in Suriname
Photo credit: Runoko Rashidi

24. Childen in Costa Chica, Mexico
Photo credit: Runoko Rashidi

The Maroons of Jamaica were fierce warriors. In 1509 Spaniards settled in Jamaica. The Spaniards had 558 enslaved Africans with them. In 1655, the British attacked the settlement and many of the enslaved Africans escaped to the mountains. They were given the name Maroon, which means African descendants brought together in a struggle for freedom. They were organized and skilled at fighting in mountain areas. Two main groups among the Maroons were called the Leeward and the Windward, based on their locations in the western and eastern parts of the island of Jamaica. The most memorable leaders are Captain Cudjoe and Queen Nanny.

The Maroons were a diverse group of Africans and most were of West African heritage. Their belief system was that of the Akans of present day Ghana and Cote d'Ivoire. The Maroons held African women in high regard. Though the Maroons were eventually forced to negotiate with the British, they will be remembered for resisting the British desire to control their lives.

Now we meet Queen Nanny, known as the mother of all Jamaicans – she is a national hero. Nanny Town was founded in 1720. Between 1725 and 1740 she led the Maroons' resistance to the British. Nanny organized and led fighting campaigns. For over 150 years Maroons helped to free enslaved Africans from European-owned plantations. Jamaica's Maroon war was such an important example of Black power. The Maroon town of Accompong has had the longest period of sovereignty within a nation dating back from the 1730's until today and this is still recognized to be true.

As we advance our journey, we continue to cross the Caribbean Sea to Haiti. For thirteen years, with the help of Maroons who lived in the mountains, the Black people fought for sovereignty and freedom from the French. Toussaint L'Ouverture led these Africans in the fight to end slavery. With his help, they stood against their former oppressors and declared independence, taking control of the island in a fierce and brutal struggle and defeating the three great empires of the time, Spain, Britain and France.

In 1804 Jean-Jacques Dessalines announced the creation of Haiti, a new nation established by former enslaved Africans of colony the French called Saint Dominique. Jean Jacques Dessalines said, "Never again will a European colonist set foot on the territory of Haiti as a master or proprietor." By declaring their independence, the people of Haiti solidified their place in African history. The first truly free society and the first sovereign Black nation in the Americas.

In the United States we meet a Black woman named Harriet Tubman who had been enslaved since her birth in 1823. She led over three hundred Black men and women to freedom. She served as a nurse and was an agent for the Union army during the Civil War. Harriet Tubman said, "I was conductor of the Underground Railroad for eight years, and I can say what most conductors can't say – I never ran my train off the track and I never lost a passenger."

In addition to great African-American freedom fighters like Harriet Tubman, a number of African-Americans excelled in the field of science and invention. Lewis Latimer was an African-American inventor, engineer, author, poet and musician. Among his inventions, was a light bulb which used a filament of a more durable carbon compared to the one Thomas Edison used. He sold the patent to the United States Electrical Company in 1881 and later went on to develop a more efficient way of manufacturing carbon filament.

25. A Black youth in Haiti
Photo credit: Runoko Rashidi

Probably even more famous was George Washington Carver. He was a chemist and botanist and found many ingenious uses for the peanut.

And there was Ernest Everett Just, a pioneering marine biologist.

Another African-American scientist, Elijah J. McCoy, was an inventor of such accomplishment that he is called the Real McCoy!

In August 1887 Marcus Garvey was born in St. Ann's Bay, Jamaica. Garvey became one of our greatest leaders and assembled the largest Black organization ever.

26. A mosaic of Marcus Gavey in Kingston, Jamaica
Photo credit: Runoko Rashidi

Garvey? Hmm... what a powerful name... sounds so familiar.

Yes it is a powerful name, for a powerful man and a powerful little girl.

What was his organization called?

That organization is called the Universal Negro Improvement Association & African Communities League. A few years ago I was named the official Traveling Ambassador of the UNIA & ACL.

Some people say that it was a "Back to Africa" movement but it was much more than that. It was designed to create Black pride, Black unity, and jobs for Black people. The slogan "Africa for the Africans: Those at Home and those Abroad" was a rallying point used to bring Black people together. Marcus Garvey stated "The Black skin is not a badge of shame, but rather a glorious symbol of national greatness."

We have a vast history, the greatest story that has barely been told. It is up to us to learn and retell our stories as our ancestors did before us.

There are other parts of the Americas that I have visited that we have barely talked about.

Africans in Brazil make it the largest concentration of Black people in the Americas. Tens of millions of Black people live there, especially in states like Bahia. It is almost like being in Africa itself! Brazil was colonized by the Portuguese and slavery was only abolished there in the 1880s. There is still a lot of prejudice and racism against Black people there. The greatest African in the history of Brazil is Zumbi. He is the greatest freedom fighter in the history of that country.

Cuba, the Dominican Republic and Puerto Rico in the Caribbean also have large African populations. In 1843, an African woman in Cuba called Carlota Lukumi helped lead a revolt of enslaved Africans. The island of Puerto Rico had many rebellions of enslaved Africans.

Grenada, in the Caribbean, produced the revolutionary African-Caribbean leader Maurice Bishop.

Today, large African populations live in Colombia and Panama. In Colombia the African population is very large, probably at least a third of the total population. The Central American countries, Honduras, Costa Rica and Nicaragua have sizable African populations. Many of the Black people there came from some of the English speaking islands in the Caribbean. Even Guatemala has a small Black population.

In South America there are Black communities in Venezuela, Peru, Ecuador and Bolivia. Former Venezuelan president, Hugo Chavez, famously boasted that he had African ancestry.

The history of African people in Argentina, Chile, Paraguay and Uruguay deserves more study. But even now you can find African people in all of these countries. It is said that during the nineteenth century Africans in Buenos Aires, the capital of Argentina, invented the dance called the Tango.

There is only one English-speaking country in South America. It is the country of Guyana and has produced a lot of great African activists and scholars. George G.M. James who wrote a book called *Stolen Legacy* (about the Greek theft of African philosophy) was from Guyana. Guyana also produced the man named Walter Rodney. Dr. Rodney wrote an important book called *How Europe Underdeveloped Africa?* Guyana also produced my greatest teacher. His name was Ivan Van Sertima and he became famous for writing and speaking about Africans in ancient America. His most important book is called *They Came Before Columbus*.

27. A young Black woman in Colombia
Photo credit: Runoko Rashidi

28. A statue of Caspar Yanga in Yanga, Mexico
Photo credit: Runoko Rashidi

29. Two girls in El Carmen, Peru
Photo credit: Runoko Rashidi

30. A Garifuna girl in Sambo Creek, Honduras
Photo credit: Runoko Rashidi

In North America, even now, Mexico has millions of African people. A great Mexican freedom fighter was a man named Gaspar Yanga. Today there is a town in the state of Vera Cruz named after him. Whenever I take a group to Mexico, I take them to Yanga do a libation ceremony in his honour and in his name. The second president of Mexico was a Black man named Vicente Guerrero. Today, an entire state in Mexico is named after him!

In Bermuda, in the North Atlantic, and in many of the large cities of Canada, sizable Black communities exist.

The most famous African in the history of Bermuda is Sally Bassett. About four-hundred years ago she was accused to giving poison to the enslaved Africans to kill the slave-owners. There is a bronze statue of her today in Hamilton, Bermuda.

In Canada, the first African that we know of was Mathieu de Costa, who visited Nova Scotia more than four-hundred years ago. It was also in Canada that Marcus Garvey made one of his last great speeches. In this speech he exclaimed, in words that are now famous, "none but ourselves can free the mind!"

Just the beginning!

So Assata-Garvey, that is a little bit of our story, the story of the African Diaspora or what I call the Global African Community. Did you like it?

Yes, Dad, I loved it! And I really loved the pictures! I am proud of you! You have seen the whole world it seems!

Yes, honey, I have seen a lot of the world. I have been very blessed. We have the greatest story that has barely been told. I'm so happy you let me share some of it with you. Maybe next time you will let me tell you about Africa itself.

Yes, Dad! I would like that very much.

Next time Assata-Garvey. Next time!

Activity 1: The Global African Presence In Asia
Complete the Ancestors Honour Scroll List

Directions: Welcome to The Global African Presence celebration! We are glad you have taken the journey. Now it's time to celebrate our ancestors! But wait! I have an important job for you. The scroll needs to be completed with the names of our great Ancestors. Read the facts below and you will know the names needed to complete our Ancestors Honour Scroll list, which will be read at the celebration. Turn back to the African Diaspora in Asia section for reminders if you need to.

1. The Sumerians helped introduce astronomy, mathematics, and pharmacies to the world. Name two of its great leaders: _____

2. This Great Queen ruled the Kingdom of Saba, in the Southwest part of the Arabian Peninsula: _____

3. This Prince responsible for the spread of martial arts from Southern India to China: _____

4. Rome's most famous Egyptian born knight: _____

5. The greatest Australian resistance leader: _____

6. The first Shogun of Japan; tradition states that this great Shogun was Black: _____

7. The Yuan Dynasty of China was started by this Mongolian conqueror: _____

Activity 2: The Global African Presence In Europe

Directions: Locate and circle the words in the list below on the graph. The words can be forward, backward, or diagonal.

```
U M V K B L A C K M A D O N N A E W B D
A O W I W P V I R I K T O N E H G G L I
E A N E V R U C B D H E J X R P D T A A
T F Z A P N S V X G Z J L V E U T V C S
S S E U R O P E I G G R U I S O R F K P
B X U L G I Q N Z G O S P V I A J P S O
H I D R Z R K E R M N R R R X P K U A R
P Y Y X E K O P E A V J P S Y X R S I A
X M T Q C V M N C H Y W C O O S Q H N U
D S U A H X E I K A C B G G F V Q K T W
M B L E E S R S E T R U S C A N M I H O
D B F B S F X A S P G K K W X B B N C A
D U Z R A U B F F U Z Z R U S S I A J G
E D M X I Y M D E C I R U A M T S K I E
B X H A E C E E R G Q M I F R S Q I U F
M O O R S M G G M F D M I V N A Z H P F
X C U D K R Y L A T I D Z T J Z M A G I
T Z N G D A R K A G E S O N P H V A O V
K Y R S F F Y I B E L T S A C E H G B G
R B J A R X C T E B V R G I B J S G F H
```

ROME
ITALY
STMAURICE
ETRUSCAN
MOORS
MUSEUM
CASTLE
EUROPE
DIASPORA
RUSSIA
PUSHKIN
MAGI
BLACKKNIGHT
GREECE
DARKAGES
AFRICANS
DUMAS
BLACKMADONNA
BLACKSAINT
SEPTIMIUSSEVERUS

Activity 3: The Global African Presence In Australia

Find the Secret Coded Message

Directions: Fill in the blanks with the correct answers. Then, enter the letters below to match the numbers and solve the secret message. This is something very important for all Africans and Blacks in the diaspora to have in our effort to be free.

         1

1. The greatest resistance leader to fight for the Indigenous Aboriginal people in New South Wales was – – – – – – – –. (1 word; 8 letters)
         1

2. Your guide in Australia was a sister from Tasmania. What was her name? – – – – – – – – –. (1 word; 9 letters)
    2

3. Sacred sites were created when all things in nature were made. This was done in the – – – – – – – – –. (1 word; 9 letters)
      3

4. Aboriginal Australian children who were stolen from their parents are the – – – – – – – – – – – – – – – – (2 words; 6 letters and 10 letters)
    4

5. Which colour on the Aboriginal flag represents the sun, the giver of life? – – – – – –. (1 word; 6 letters)
5

The Secret Coded Message is: – – – – –!
       1 2 3 4 5

Activity 4: The Global African Presence in The Pacific Islands

Directions: Choose the items from the list of "People, Places and Events" and enter them under the correct "Three Pacific Island Chains" on the chart. Let's see what you can remember on your own, but you may turn back to the previous pages for reminders, if necessary.

People, Places, and Events

The Maori people live here	Name means the "Black Islands"	Port Moresby
Kamehameha the Great	Vanuatu cyclone	Chuuk
New Zealand or Aotearoa	Name means "the small islands"	Hawaii
Chief Benny Wenda	Palau	Chief Atai
Biggest island in New Guinea	Name means "many islands"	Blackbirding

Three Pacific Island Chains

Polynesia	Melanesia	Micronesia

Activity 5: The Global African Presence in The Americas

Directions: Locate and circle the words in the list below on the graph. The words can be forward, backward, or diagonal.

```
S E E M W V S Q M S G L S E C U D Y V F
E C O K Y C W U D L D R O M O R D O Z L
N N W M U S L E W S Y I N Z A R X Z R G
I A L D W E S E A D M E H W K S J N W X
L T S E M O R N L S N H D N I Q A E Z K
A S E L K J J N P M P N N Y C F B R F V
S I T A G D Y A V N I A A V N U U O G F
E S O T D U Y N N W M S S I Z B B L I Y
D E P I W C O N T B N A L P A L A A N S
N R A M U D L Y U A Z A R S V P K I T D
D Y Z E V T E T M L M E A O G H A Z G A
L R S R E M E U F K A L F G O N R U L E
E E E V T F W T U K T V Z Q A N I L P H
M S R H K G A Z B W I E E G D R S T C E
X R T P I M R U B K D J Q N K C V B T N
Y X I D K F D C W F A Q I V T E Y E Y O
U Z M R G T B E C U T H M K T A O Y Y T
Z N L I G H K M T O U S S A I N T Z W S
H R K W D J Y L Q R L T Y P Y E I Z A G
F Z M P K L Z O K Y O U H M Z A I Q Y U
```

OLMEC
GARVEY
CUDJOE
ABUBAKARI
LEEWARD
STONEHEADS
LATIMER
MAYA
BASALT
LUZIA
QUEENNANNY
MALI
TUBMAN
LORENZO
MANSA
WINDWARD
LAVENTA
RESISTANCE
TRESZAPOTES
MAROONS
TOUSSAINT
DESALINES

Activity 6: The Global African Presence Bonus Puzzle

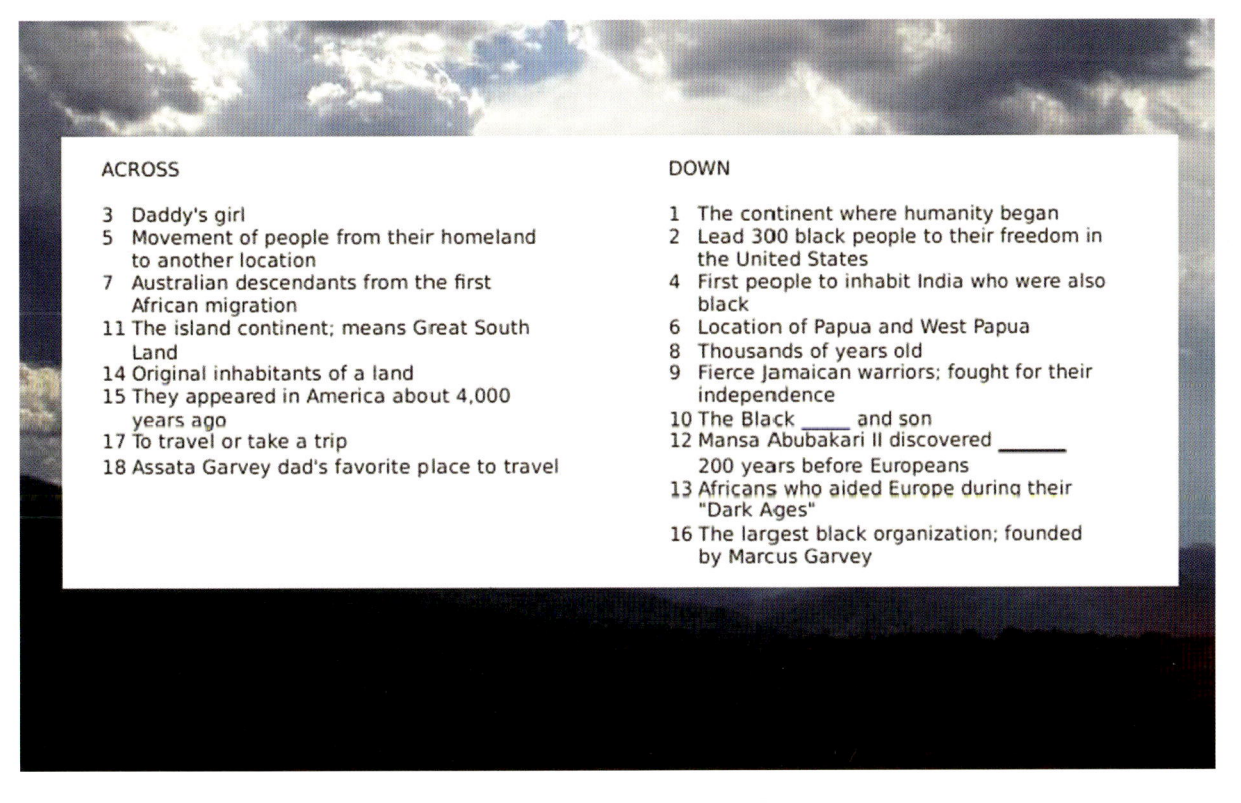

ACROSS

3. Daddy's girl
5. Movement of people from their homeland to another location
7. Australian descendants from the first African migration
11. The island continent; means Great South Land
14. Original inhabitants of a land
15. They appeared in America about 4,000 years ago
17. To travel or take a trip
18. Assata Garvey dad's favorite place to travel

DOWN

1. The continent where humanity began
2. Lead 300 black people to their freedom in the United States
4. First people to inhabit India who were also black
6. Location of Papua and West Papua
8. Thousands of years old
9. Fierce Jamaican warriors; fought for their independence
10. The Black _____ and son
12. Mansa Abubakari II discovered _____ 200 years before Europeans
13. Africans who aided Europe during their "Dark Ages"
16. The largest black organization; founded by Marcus Garvey

Key 1: The Global African Presence In Asia
Complete the Ancestors Honour Scroll List

1. The Sumerians helped introduce astronomy, mathematics, and pharmacies to the world. Name two of its great leaders: **Gudea and Kubaba**

2. This Great Queen ruled the Kingdom of Saba, in the Southwest part of the Arabian Peninsula: **Queen of Sheba**

3. This Prince responsible for the spread of martial arts from Southern India to China: **Daruma Bodhidarma**

4. Rome's most famous Egyptian born knight: **Saint Maurice**

5. The greatest Australian resistance leader: **Pemulwuy**

6. The first Shogun of Japan; tradition states that this great Shogun was Black: **Sakanouye Tamuramaro**

7. The Yuan Dynasty of China was started by this Mongolian conqueror: **Kublai Khan**

Key 2: The Global African Presence In Europe

```
U M V K B L A C K M A D O N N A E W B D
A O W I W P V I R I K T O N E H G G L I
E A N E V R U C B D H E J X R P D T A A
T F Z A P N S V X G Z J L V E U T V C S
S S E U R O P E I G G R U I S O R F K P
B X U L G I Q N Z G O S P V I A J P S O
H I D R Z R K E R M N R R R X P K U A R
P Y Y X E K O P E A V J P S Y X R S I A
X M T Q C V M N C H Y W C O O S Q H N U
D S U A H X E I K A C B G G F V Q K T W
M B L E E S R S E T R U S C A N M I H O
D B F S F X A S P G K K W X B B N C A
D U Z R A U B F F U Z Z R U S S I A J G
E D M X I Y M D E C I R U A M T S K I E
B X H A E C E E R G Q M I F R S Q I U F
M O O R S M G G M F D M I V N A Z H P F
X C U D K R Y L A T I D Z T J Z M A G I
T Z N G D A R K A G E S O N P H V A O V
K Y R S F F Y I B E L T S A C E H G B G
R B J A R X C T E B V R G I B J S G F H
```

ROME
ITALY
STMAURICE
ETRUSCAN
MOORS
MUSEUM
CASTLE
EUROPE
DIASPORA
RUSSIA
PUSHKIN
MAGI
BLACKKNIGHT
GREECE
DARKAGES
AFRICANS
DUMAS
BLACKMADONNA
BLACKSAINT
SEPTIMIUSSEVERUS

Key 3: The Global African Presence in Australia

1. The greatest resistance leader to fight for the Indigenous Aboriginal people in New South Wales was <u>P E M U L W U Y</u>. (1 word; 8 letters)
                  1

2. Your guide in Australia was a sister from Tasmania. What was her name? <u>T R U G A N I N I</u>. (1 word; 9 letters)
        2

3. Sacred sites were created when all things in nature were made. This was done in the <u>D R E A M T I M E</u>. (1 word; 9 letters)
             3

4. Aboriginal Australian children who were stolen from their parents are the <u>S T O L E N G E N E R A T I O N</u>. (2 words; 6 letters and 10 letters)
                4

5. Which colour on the Aboriginal flag represents the sun, the giver of life? <u>Y E L L O W</u>. (1 word; 6 letters)
5

The Secret Coded Message is: <u>U N I T Y</u>!
                                   1 2 3 4 5

Key 4: The Global African Presence in The Pacific Islands

Three Pacific Island Chains

Polynesia	Melanesia	Micronesia
Name means "many islands"	Name means the "Black Islands"	Name means "the small islands"
New Zealand or Aotearoa	Vanuatu cyclone	Palau
Hawaii	Biggest island in New Guinea	Chuuk
Kamehameha the Great	Port Moresby	
The Maori people live here	Chief Benny Wenda	
	Blackbirding	
	Chief Atai	

Key 5: The Global African Presence in The Americas

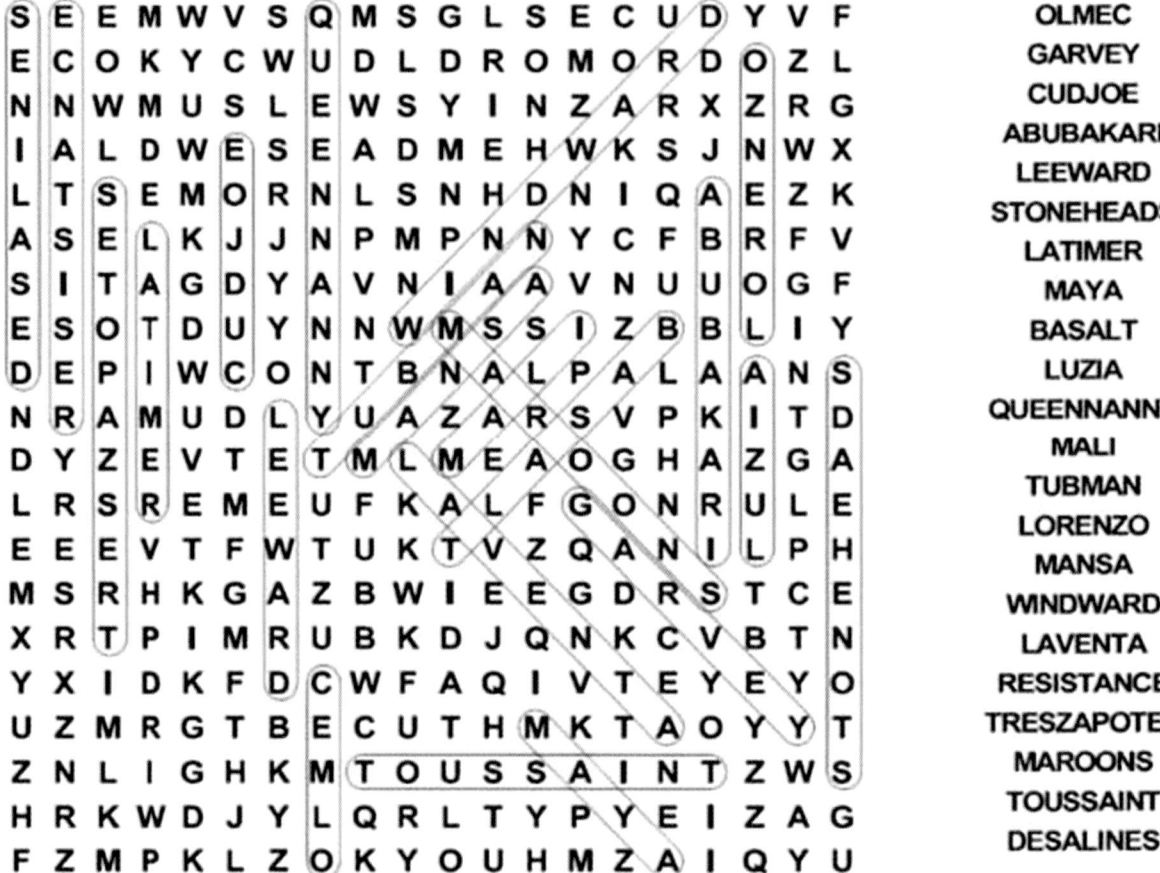

```
S E E M W V S Q M S G L S E C U D Y V F
E C O K Y C W U D L D R O M O R D O Z L
N N W M U S L E W S Y I N Z A R X Z R G
I A L D W E S E A D M E H W K S J N W X
L T S E M O R N L S N H D N I Q A E Z K
A S E L K J J N P M P N Y C F B R F V
S I T A G D Y A V N I A A V N U U O G F
E S O T D U Y N N W M S S I Z B B L I Y
D E P I W C O N T B N A L P A L A A N S
N R A M U D L Y U A Z A R S V P K I T D
D Y Z E V T E T M L M E A O G H A Z G A
L R S R E M E U F K A L F G O N R U L E
E E E V T F W T U K T V Z Q A N I L P H
M S R H K G A Z B W I E E G D R S T C E
X R T P I M R U B K D J Q N K C V B T N
Y X I D K F D C W F A Q I V T E Y E Y O
U Z M R G T B E C U T H M K T A O Y Y T
Z N L I G H K M T O U S S A I N T Z W S
H R K W D J Y L Q R L T Y P Y E I Z A G
F Z M P K L Z O K Y O U H M Z A I Q Y U
```

OLMEC
GARVEY
CUDJOE
ABUBAKARI
LEEWARD
STONEHEADS
LATIMER
MAYA
BASALT
LUZIA
QUEENNANNY
MALI
TUBMAN
LORENZO
MANSA
WINDWARD
LAVENTA
RESISTANCE
TRESZAPOTES
MAROONS
TOUSSAINT
DESALINES

Key 6: The Global African Presence Bonus Puzzle

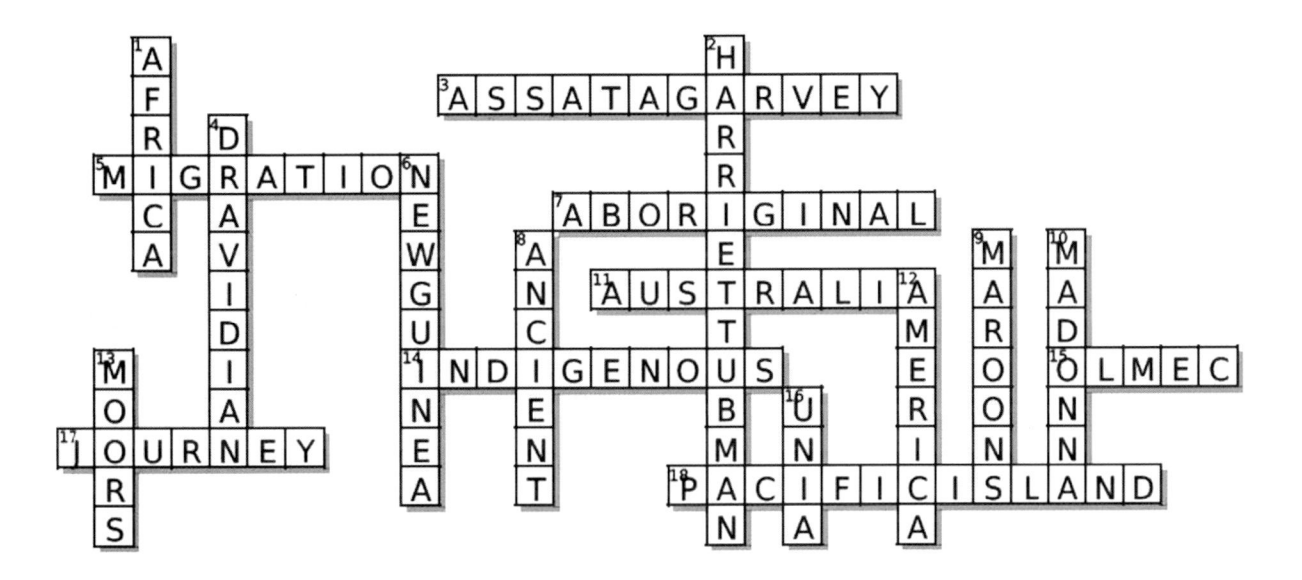

```
        A
        F
        R         D
      M I G R A T I O N        H
        C       A     E    A S S A T A G A R V E Y
        A       V     W         R
                I     G    A    R
                D     U    N  A B O R I G I N A L
                I     I    C    E
              M O     N  A U S T R A L I A  M    M
              O       E    E         M   A    A
              O       A    N         E   R  O L M E C
        J O U R N E Y   T  B  U      R   O    N
        R               M  N         I   O    N
        S             P A C I F I C I S L A N D
                        N  A
```

Annexes

Annex 1: Black people all over the world

Modern names of countries marked on the map. (Old names in brackets.)

1. Andaman Islands
2. Malaysia, Thailand
3. Philippines
4. Iraq (Sumer, Mesopotamia)
5. Ethiopia
6. India
7. Sri Lanka
8. Pakistan
9. Turkey (Ottoman Empire)
10. China
11. Japan
12. Arabia
13. Cambodia
14. Vietnam
15. Egypt (Kmt)
16. Sudan (Nubia)
17. Crete, Greece
18. Morocco
19. France
20. UK, England
21. Russia
22. Australia
23. Tasmania
24. Solomon Islands
25. New Caledonia
26. Vanuatu
27. Fiji
28. Papua New Guinea
29. New Zealand (Aoteroa)
30. Mexico (Olmec)
31. Guatemala (Maya)
32. Cuba
33. Guyana
34. Brazil
35. Grenada
36. Jamaica
37. Haiti
38. USA
39. Venezuela
40. Colombia
41. Peru
42. Bolivia
43. Canada
44. Zanzibar

Annex 2: Dr Runoko's global travels map

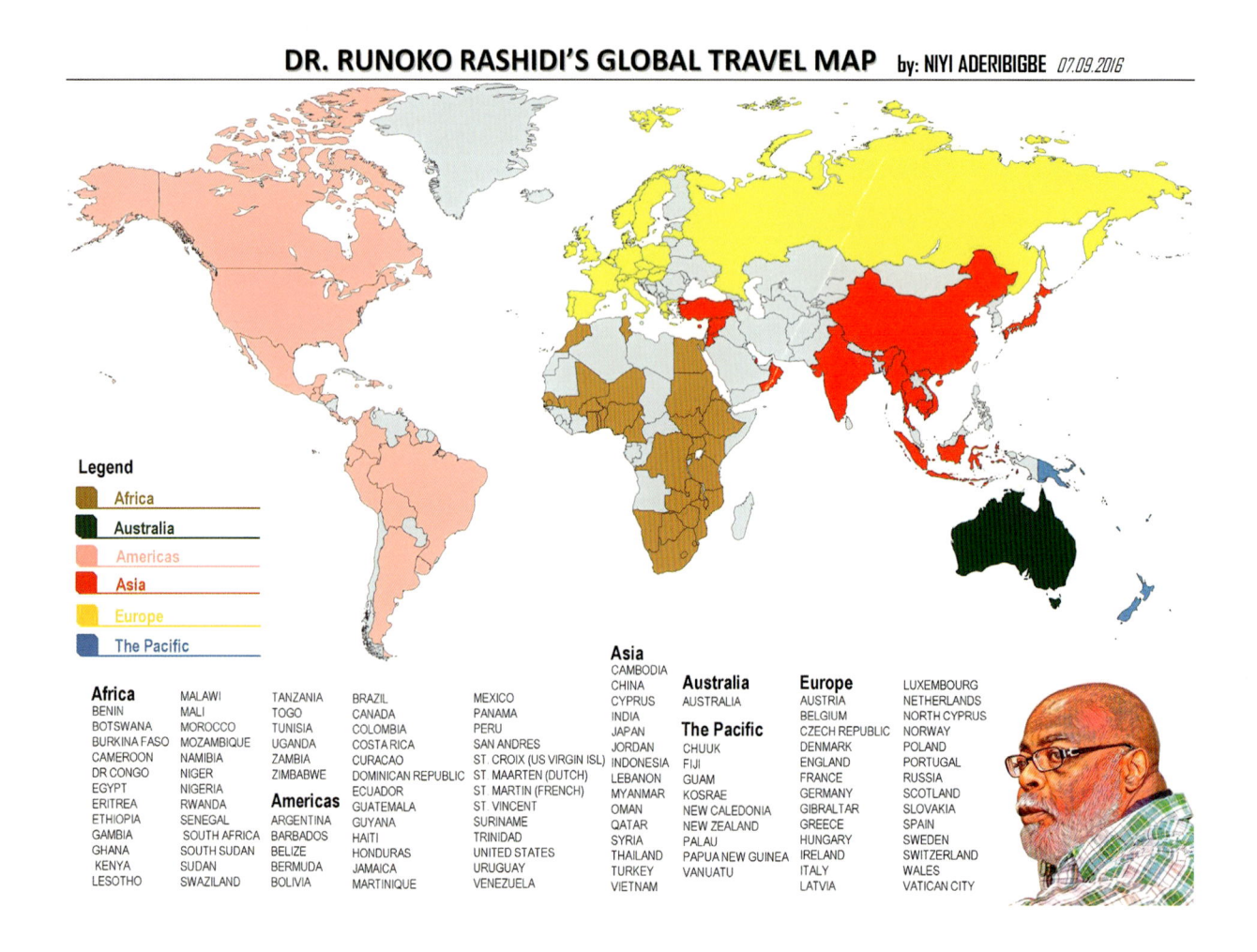

DR. RUNOKO RASHIDI'S GLOBAL TRAVEL MAP
by: NIYI ADERIBIGBE 07.09.2016

Legend
- Africa
- Australia
- Americas
- Asia
- Europe
- The Pacific

Africa
BENIN
BOTSWANA
BURKINA FASO
CAMEROON
DR CONGO
EGYPT
ERITREA
ETHIOPIA
GAMBIA
GHANA
KENYA
LESOTHO
MALAWI
MALI
MOROCCO
MOZAMBIQUE
NAMIBIA
NIGER
NIGERIA
RWANDA
SENEGAL
SOUTH AFRICA
SOUTH SUDAN
SUDAN
SWAZILAND
TANZANIA
TOGO
TUNISIA
UGANDA
ZAMBIA
ZIMBABWE

Americas
ARGENTINA
BARBADOS
BELIZE
BERMUDA
BOLIVIA
BRAZIL
CANADA
COLOMBIA
COSTA RICA
CURACAO
DOMINICAN REPUBLIC
ECUADOR
GUATEMALA
GUYANA
HAITI
HONDURAS
JAMAICA
MARTINIQUE
MEXICO
PANAMA
PERU
SAN ANDRES
ST. CROIX (US VIRGIN ISL)
ST. MAARTEN (DUTCH)
ST. MARTIN (FRENCH)
ST. VINCENT
SURINAME
TRINIDAD
UNITED STATES
URUGUAY
VENEZUELA

Asia
CAMBODIA
CHINA
CYPRUS
INDIA
JAPAN
JORDAN
INDONESIA
LEBANON
MYANMAR
OMAN
QATAR
SYRIA
THAILAND
TURKEY
VIETNAM

Australia
AUSTRALIA

The Pacific
CHUUK
FIJI
GUAM
KOSRAE
NEW CALEDONIA
NEW ZEALAND
PALAU
PAPUA NEW GUINEA
VANUATU

Europe
AUSTRIA
BELGIUM
CZECH REPUBLIC
DENMARK
ENGLAND
FRANCE
GERMANY
GIBRALTAR
GREECE
HUNGARY
IRELAND
ITALY
LATVIA
LUXEMBOURG
NETHERLANDS
NORTH CYPRUS
NORWAY
POLAND
PORTUGAL
RUSSIA
SCOTLAND
SLOVAKIA
SPAIN
SWEDEN
SWITZERLAND
WALES
VATICAN CITY

Annex 3

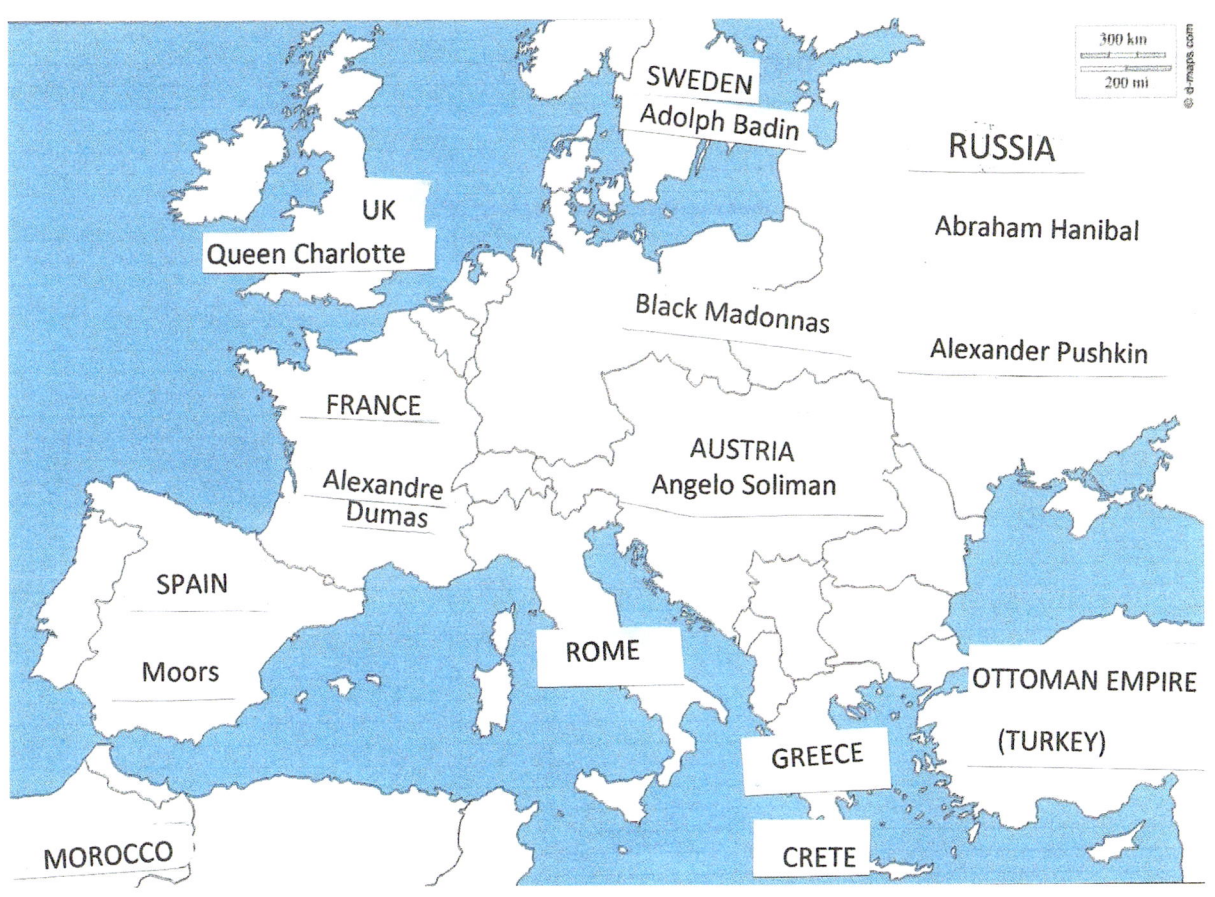

31. Map of places in Europe where Runoko has met or documented Black people

Liste of captions

1. Runoko Rashidi and a Black man from Bangladesh, in Muscat, Oman 12
2. One of the entrances to the city of Angkor Thom at Siem Reap, Cambodia 13
3. A Munda boy in Orissa, India 14
4. An Africoid figurine – perhaps an acrobat or adancer from the Tang Dynasty in China. In the Smithsonian Collection in Washington 15
5. A Buddha from early Thailand - Musee Guimet 16
6. A Khmer girl in Siem Reap, Cambodia.. 16
7. The head of the African emperor of Rome Septimius Severus 17
8. A Black person from the Etruscan civilization of early Italy 17
9. Saint Maurice – the knight in shining armour 18
10. Runoko Rashidi and a portrait of Alexander Sergeivich Pushkin in Moscow, Russia 18
11. A Black Madonna and Child in Prague, Czech Republic 19
12. Canada Toronto fine arts (17) 19
13. A bronze bust of a Moorish girl in Italy 19
14. Runoko Rashidi and with a group of Black women in Turkey 19
15. Runoko Rashidi with two Indigenous Elders in Townsville, Queensland, Australia 23
16. An Aboriginal Australian boy on Palm Island, Queensland, Australia 23
17. An Indigenous Australian woman on Palm Island Queensland – Australia 24
18. A young boy with blond hair in Fiji 28
19. A young boy on Bougainville Island, Papua New Guinea 29
20. Young boys on Buka Island, Papua New Guinea 30
21. A statue of King Kamehemeha the Great in Hilo, Hawaii 31
22. One of the Olmec Heads in Mexico 32
23. A little Saamaka girl in Suriname 33
24. Childen in Costa Chica, Mexico 33
25. A Black youth in Haiti 35
26. A mosaic of Marcus Gavey in Kingston, Jamaica 35
27. A young Black woman in Colombia... 37
28. A statue of Caspar Yanga in Yanga, Mexico 37
29. Two girls in El Carmen, Peru... 37
30. A Garifuna girl in Sambo Creek, Honduras.. 37
31. Map of places in Europe where Runoko has met or documented Black people............ 55

Glossary

Aboriginal or Indigenous: Being the first of its kind present in a region. Aboriginal people are the first inhabitants of a country.

Activist: Advocating or opposing a cause or issue vigorously, especially a political cause.

Adivasis/Tribals: Original inhabitants of India.

Aeta: A term used, not always positively, for some of the Black people that live in the northern part of the Philippines on the island of Luzon.

Africa: Africa is the birthplace of humankind. Africa is the second largest continent in the world. It is 11.67 million miles. It has 1.111 billion people.

African: People who live in Africa or trace their ancestry to the indigenous inhabitants of Africa.

Agriculture: The science of working with the earth and animals to grow foods. (Farming)

Akan: A people, culture and language of West Africa, especially Ghana and Ivory Coast.

Americas: Known as the Western Hemisphere which is made up of territories in North America, Central America, the Caribbean and South America.

Ancestors: A person from whom one is descended; the people of your family or culture that came before you that are no longer living.

Ancient: Very old: having lived or existed for a very long time or having existed a long time ago.

Angkor: The heart of the Khmer Kingdom. A Khmer word, based on the Indian Sanskrit meaning the "city" or the "capital."

Anthropology: The study of humankind.

Archaeology: Study of the material traces of the human past.

Arrested: To stop the movement of something.

Artefact: Any object made by humans.

Assemble: To build by bringing together or putting together.

Asia: The largest continent in the eastern and northern hemispheres. 44,579,000 square miles.

Australia: A country and continent surrounded by the Indian and Pacific oceans.

B.C.E.: Before the Common Era (sometimes written as B.C.).

B.P.: Before the present.

Black Madonna: Statue or painting of a Black mother and child that represent Mary and the infant Jesus.

Black Panther Party: Founded in 1966 in Oakland, California by Huey Newton and Bobby Seale to serve and protect the Black community.

Black Power Movement: A movement by Black people especially in the 1950s and 1960s more uncompromising than the U.S. Civil Rights Movement.

Boomerang: A curved wooden tool that, when thrown in a particular way, can return to the person that threw it. Widely used in Australia.

Bushmen: A condescending European name for the San people of Southern Africa.

Caribbean: A region that has the Caribbean Sea, its islands and surrounding coasts.

Celebrate: Publicly remember with a social gathering or enjoyable activity.

Ceremony: A formal, or specific way of doing things.

China: The most populous country in East Asia, with 1,357 billion people.

Circa/Ca: Approximately.

City-State: An independent state consisting of a city and the surrounding territory.

Civilization: A well developed and organized society.

Colonization: The practice of removing indigenous people from their land and settling on it.

Colossus: An enormous statue, usually of a king and typically set up outside a temple.

Conquistador: One of the European, especially Spanish, conquerors of the Americas from the fifteenth to the eighteenth centuries.

Culture: A society that has its own beliefs, ways of life, art, music, and practices.

Dalits: The only name which India's Black Untouchables have given themselves.

Dark Ages: The period of time after the fall of the Roman Empire when Europe experienced great poverty, disease and war.

Descendants: People who are the offspring of a specific ancestor.

Diaspora: A group of people who live outside the area in which they or their ancestors lived for a long time.

Diminutive Africoids or Small Black People: The sub-division of African people known to have unusually short stature, skin-complexions that range from yellowish to dark brown, and tightly curled hair. The Diminutive Africoids or Small Black People in Africa are sometimes called *Pygmies*.

Dinknesh: The skeleton remains of a 3.4 million human-like woman in Ethiopia.

DNA (Deoxyribonucleic acid): An essential chemical matter that carries genetic information passed from one generation to the next in all living things.

Domesticated: To convert animals or plants for human uses; to tame.

Dravidian: A family of languages which spread in ancient times from southern India to eastern Iraq. It was likely the language of the Harappan civilization. It also refers to many of the people of Southern India.

Dravidians: The ancient people of India.

Dynasty: A line of rulers belonging to the same family; also the period during which a certain family reigns.

Empire: A major political unit having a territory of great extent or a number of territories or peoples under a single government authority; also the period during which such a government prevails.

Exile: Separated from his or her country or home. It can be done voluntarily, by force, or due to circumstances.

Filament: Very fine thread or threadlike structure; fibre.

Forge: To form or create something through great effort: To form something by heating and shaping metal.

Fossil: Any hardened remains or traces of plant or animal life of previous geological periods, preserved in rock formations in the earth's crust.

Funan: The Chinese name for an early kingdom in Cambodia that preceded the kingdom of Angkor.

Global Warming: A gradual increase in the earth's air temperature which causes corresponding climate changes.

Harappan Civilization or Indus Valley Civilization: The high culture of the ancient Indus Valley in what is now Pakistan and related places in northwest India dating from circa 2700 B.C.E. to 1500 B.C.E.

Heritage: Inheritance which is set aside or preserved for an individual or group of people or ancestry of any people.

Hieroglyphs: "Sacred Signs"; the name associated by the early Greeks with the ancient Kamite system of 'picture writing.'

Homo sapiens sapiens: Modern human beings.

Hydraulic: Operated through the use of water.

Icon: A symbol of veneration.

Isthmus: A narrow strip of land connecting two masses of land that would otherwise be separated by water.

Independence Movement: The fight for freedom from control, influence, support, and aid from others, usually from a different country or entity.

Isolation: The separation of one nation from other nations.

Invaders: People who enter a foreign land to take possession; to enter forcefully with hostile intent.

Khmer: Referring to the people, language and culture of the civilization of Cambodia and especially Angkor.

Kmt: The African name for Ancient Egypt.

Language Family: A group of languages related through descent from a common origin.

Libation ceremony: A libation ceremony is a traditional African ceremony where drink is poured on the ground on formal occasions that calls on the spirits of our great ancestors to bless us and give us protection and success.

Linguistics: The study of human speech including the units, nature, structure and modification of language.

Lithic: Of, or pertaining to stone.

Littoral: Near, or along a coast.

Luzia: The skeletal remains of a Black woman who lived in Brazil more than ten-thousand years ago. Considered the first person in the Americas.

Mansa: The emperor or ruler of the Mali Empire in West Africa.

Material Culture: The tangible objects produced by a society.

Matrifocal: The strong presence and importance of the mother.

Megalithic: Constructed of large stones.

Migration: To move from one country or place to live or work in another.

Mongoloid: Term commonly used to describe the people of East Asia.

Monolith: A single gigantic stone or similarly huge object, often in the form of an obelisk or column.

Moors: Black people from North Africa best known as the people that conquered Spain in 711 C.E. and who laid the foundations for the introduction and advancement in Dark Age Europe of such things as astronomy, chemistry, mathematics, physics, geography, medicine and philosophy.

Mummy: The body of a deceased person wrapped up in tight bandages of cloth.

Ottoman Empire: The time of Muslim rule from Turkey for hundreds of years from around 1300 to 1920.

Prehistoric: The period before written history.

Proto: The first in time, original, principal.

Proverbs: A popular saying that gives advice or shares a belief that is thought to be true.

Region: A specific part of a country or of the world, that is different or separate from another part.

Resistance: The effort made to stop or fight against someone or something.

Riverine: On, or near, the banks of a river.

Saint: A person of great moral excellence; goodness; righteousness.

Shang: The first historical dynasty of China, from about 1800 B.C.E. to about 1060 B.C.E.

Shogun: Name given to the ancient military governors of Japan.

Siddis: A term applied to Africans and the descendants of enslaved Africans in India.

Sovereignty: Supreme and independent power or authority in government.

Spirituality: Having a personal understanding of the creator of all things: Showing respect for life, nature, ancestors and the inner quality or nature of a person.

Stela: A stone column or upright slab decorated with carvings or inscriptions.

Steppe: Vast grasslands capable of supporting herds of grazing animals, but generally too cold and arid for the growing of crops.

Underground Railroad: The Underground Railroad was the method of escape and the escape route taken by enslaved Africans in the southern part of the United States to freedom in the north and to Canada.

Wat: In Southeast Asia a Buddhist temple or religious complex.

Zanj: The name of the African people from East Africa who were taken to Iraq for hundreds of years and who participated in the largest rebellion of enslaved people in history.

Ziggurat: Massive rectangular shaped, step-temple structures or stage-towers in early Western Asia, generally composed of mud bricks.

For further reading

Clarke, John Henrik, editor. *Marcus Garvey and the Vision of Africa*. Baltimore: Black Classic Press, 2014.

Elder, Bruce. *Blood on the Wattle: The Massacre and Maltreatment of Aboriginal Australians since 1788*. Sydney: New Holland Publishers, 1998.

Gnammankou, Dieudonné. *Abraham Hannibal: Pushkin's African Ancestor*. London: Books of Africa, Ltd., 2015.

Imhotep, David. *The First Americans were Africans: Documented Evidence*. Bloomington: AuthorHouse, 2011.

Katz, William Loren. *Black Indians: A Hidden History*. New York: Atheneum, 1986.

Price, Richard, editor. *Maroon Societies: Rebel Slave Communities in the Americas*. Baltimore: John Hopkins University Press, 1996.

Rashidi, Runoko. *Black Star: The African Presence in Early Europe*. London: Books of Africa, Ltd. 2012.

Rashidi, Runoko. *African Star over Asia: The Black Presence in the East*. London: Books of Africa, Ltd., 2013.

Rashidi, Runoko. *Uncovering the African Past: The Ivan Van Sertima Papers*. London: Books of Africa, Ltd., 2015.

Raven, Susan. *Rome in Africa*. London: Routledge, 1993.

Scobie, Edward. *Global African Presence*. Brooklyn: A&B Books, 1994.

Turnbull, Ryan. *The Aboriginal Tasmanians*. Crows Nest, NSW: Allen & Unwin, 1996.

Van Sertima, Ivan. *They Came Before Columbus: The African Presence in Ancient America*. New York: Random House, 1976.

Van Sertima, Ivan, editor. *Blacks in Science: Ancient and Modern*. New Brunswick: Transaction Press, 1983.

Van Sertima, Ivan, editor. *African Presence in Early Europe*. New Brunswick: Transaction Press, 1985.

Van Sertima, Ivan, editor. *Golden Age of the Moor*. New Brunswick: Transaction Press, 1992.

Williams, Chancellor. *Destruction of Black Civilization: Great Issues of a Race from 4500 BC to 2000 AD*. Chicago: Third World Press, 1973.